This Book Belongs To

MAXend   SOPHIA

Mr. Funny

Little Miss Giggles

MR. MEN™
LITTLE MISS™
Giant Book of Doodles and Fun

Little Miss Sunshine

Mr. Happy

PSS!
PRICE STERN SLOAN
An Imprint of Penguin Group (USA) Inc.

MR. MEN   LITTLE MISS

PSS!
PRICE STERN SLOAN

Table of Contents

Meet the Mr. Men and Little Misses!

 Mr. Tickle

Mr. Greedy

Mr. Happy

 Mr. Nosey

Mr. Sneeze

Mr. Bump

Mr. Snow

 Mr. Messy

Mr. Topsy-Turvy

 Mr. Silly

Mr. Uppity

Mr. Small

Mr. Daydream

Mr. Forgetful

Mr. Nervous

Mr. Noisy

Mr. Lazy

 Mr. Funny

 Mr. Stingy

Mr. Chatterbox

 Mr. Fussy

Mr. Bounce

Mr. Muddle

Mr. Dizzy

Mr. Impossible

Mr. Strong

 Mr. Grumpy

Mr. Clumsy

 Mr. Quiet

 Mr. Rush

Mr. Tall

 Mr. Worry

Mr. Nonsense

 Mr. Wrong

 Mr. Skinny

 Mr. Mischief

Mr. Clever

 Mr. Busy

 Mr. Slow

Mr. Brave

 Mr. Grumble

 Mr. Perfect

6

 Mr. Cheerful

 Mr. Cool

 Mr. Rude

 Mr. Good

 Mr. Nobody

 Little Miss Bossy

 Little Miss Naughty

 Little Miss Neat

 Little Miss Sunshine

Little Miss Tiny

Little Miss Trouble

 Little Miss Giggles

 Little Miss Helpful

 Little Miss Magic

 Little Miss Shy

Little Miss Splendid

Little Miss Twins

 Little Miss Chatterbox

 Little Miss Ditzy

 Little Miss Late

 Little Miss Lucky

Little Miss Scatterbrain

Little Miss Star

 Little Miss Busy

 Little Miss Quick

 Little Miss Wise

 Little Miss Tidy

Little Miss Greedy

 Little Miss Fickle

 Little Miss Brainy

 Little Miss Stubborn

 Little Miss Curious

 Little Miss Fun

 Little Miss Contrary

 Little Miss Somersault

 Little Miss Scary

 Little Miss Bad

 Little Miss Whoops

 Little Miss Princess

little Miss Sunshine

by Roger Hargreaves

Welcome to Miseryland.

We say "Welcome," but there really isn't very much welcoming about it.

It's the most miserable place in the world.

Miseryland worms look like this!

And when the birds wake up in the morning in Miseryland, they don't start singing.

They start crying!

Oh, it really is an awful place!

And the king of Miseryland is even worse.

He sits on his throne all day long with tears streaming down his face.

"Oh, I'm so unhappy," he keeps sobbing over and over and over again.

Dear, oh dear, oh dear!

Little Miss Sunshine had been on vacation.

She'd had a lovely time, and now she was driving home.

She was whistling happily to herself as she drove along when, out of the corner of her eye, she saw a sign.

TO MISERYLAND.

"Miseryland?" she asked herself. "I've never heard of that before!"

And she headed down the road leading to Miseryland.

She came to a sign that read:

YOU ARE NOW ENTERING MISERYLAND
    SMILING
    LAUGHING
    CHUCKLING
    GIGGLING
FORBIDDEN
By Order of the King.

Oh dear, thought Little Miss Sunshine as she drove along.

She came to a castle with a huge door.

A soldier stopped her.

"What do you want?" he asked gloomily.

"I want to see the king," smiled Little Miss Sunshine.

"You're under arrest," said the soldier.

"But why?" asked Little Miss Sunshine.

"For a very serious crime," replied the soldier. "Very serious indeed!"

The soldier marched Little Miss Sunshine through the huge door.

And across a courtyard.

And through another huge door.

And up an enormous staircase.

And along a long corridor.

And through another huge door.

And into a gigantic room.

And at the end of the gigantic room sat the king.

Crying his eyes out!

"Your Majesty," said the soldier, bowing low. "I have arrested this person for a very serious crime!"

The king stopped crying.

"She smiled at me," said the soldier.

There was a shocked silence.

"She did WHAT?" cried the king.

"She smiled at me," repeated the soldier.

"But why is smiling not allowed?" laughed Little Miss Sunshine.

"She LAUGHED at me!" cried the king.

"Why not?" she chuckled.

"She CHUCKLED!" wailed the king.

Little Miss Sunshine giggled.

"She GIGGLED!" blubbered the king.

And he burst into tears again.

"But why are these things not allowed?" asked Little Miss Sunshine.

"Because this is Miseryland," wept the king. "And they've never been allowed," he sobbed. "Oh, I was so unhappy before you arrived," he wailed, "but now I'm twice as unhappy!"

Little Miss Sunshine looked at him.

"But wouldn't you like to be happy?" she asked.

"Of course I would," cried the king. "But how can I be? This is MISERYLAND!"

Little Miss Sunshine thought.

"Come on," she said.

"You can't talk to me like that," sobbed the king.

"Don't be silly," she replied, and led him across the gigantic room, and through the huge door, and along the long corridor, and down the enormous staircase, and through the huge door, and across the courtyard, and through the huge door to her car.

"Get in," she said.

Little Miss Sunshine drove the crying king back to the large Miseryland sign.

"Dry your eyes," she said, and handed him a large handkerchief from her purse.

And then, from her purse, she pulled out a large pen.

Five minutes later she'd finished.

Instead of the sign reading:

YOU ARE NOW ENTERING MISERYLAND
SMILING
LAUGHING
CHUCKLING
GIGGLING
FORBIDDEN
By Order of the King.

Do you know what it read?

YOU ARE NOW ENTERING LAUGHTERLAND
     SMILING
     LAUGHING
     CHUCKLING
     GIGGLING
PERMITTED
By Order of the King.

"There," said Little Miss Sunshine. "Now you can be happy."

"But I don't know HOW to be happy," sniffed the king. "I've never TRIED it!"

"Nonsense," said Little Miss Sunshine. "It's really very easy," she smiled.

The king tried a smile.

"Not bad," she laughed.

The king tried a laugh.

"Getting better," she chuckled.

The king tried a chuckle.

"You've got it," she giggled.

The king looked at her.

"So I have," he giggled. "I'm the king of Laughterland!"

As Little Miss Sunshine arrived home, there was Mr. Happy out for an evening stroll.

"Hello," he grinned. "Where have you been?"

"Miseryland!" she replied.

"Miseryland?" he said. "I didn't know there was such a place!"

Little Miss Sunshine giggled.

"Actually," she said.

38

"There isn't!"

Coloring and Activities

A-MAZING!

Mr. Tickle is sledding!

Can you spot the 10 differences
between these two pictures?

The string has broken on one of these balloons.
Who has lost their balloon?

Mr. Funny   Mr. Lazy   Mr. Uppity   Mr. Quiet   Mr. Stingy   Mr. Fussy

When you have worked out who has lost his balloon, draw a frown on his face, and then draw a smile on the faces of the other Mr. Men.

SECRET CODE

COLOR-BY-NUMBERS

1 = Blue
2 = Red
3 = Green
4 = Orange
5 = Yellow
6 = Brown
7 = Pink

Use the guide to color the picture.

Match the squares to the holes in the picture and draw them in so that Little Miss Somersault can get a good night's sleep.

A

B

C

CAULIFLOWERS

POTATOES

CARROTS

MATCHING

Mr. Silly has lost his right shoe.
Which is the right one?

Write the answer on his right foot!

COLOR-BY-NUMBERS

Mr. Greedy never has enough!
Use the guide to color the picture.

1=Pink, 2=Yellow,
3=Red,
4=Blue, 5=Orange

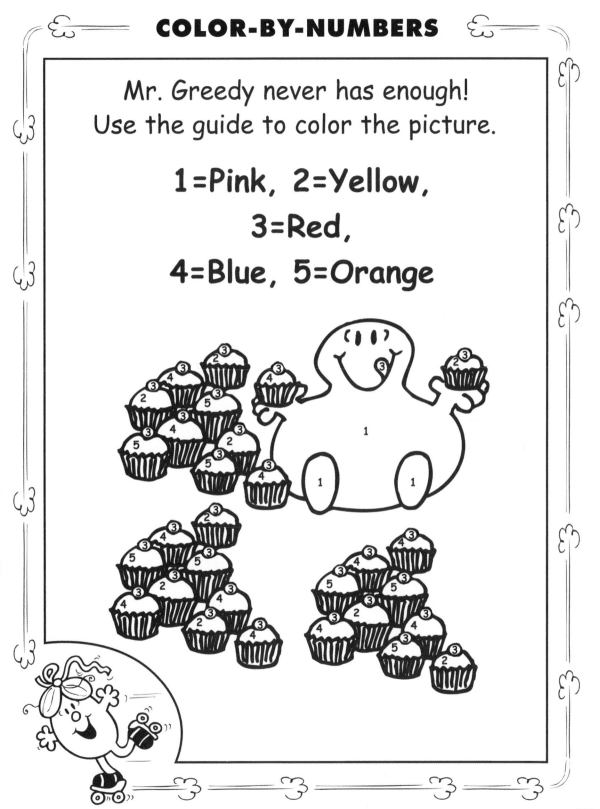

COLORING FUN

little miss Scatterbrain

A-MAZING!

Mr. Fussy

Mr. Funny

Mr. Silly

Mr. Stingy

Mr. Clever

Mr. Slow

ACHOO!

Which two Mr. Men have caught Mr. Sneeze's cold?
Complete the maze to find out.
Color their noses red!

Which Mr. Bump is the odd one out?

Which naughty Mr. Man undid Mr. Fussy's shoelace?

Mr. Happy

Mr. Clever

Mr. Funny

Mr. Mischief

Mr. Small

A-MAZING!

Mr. Small is lost in the long grass!
Can you help him find the way out?

LINES AND THE BOXES

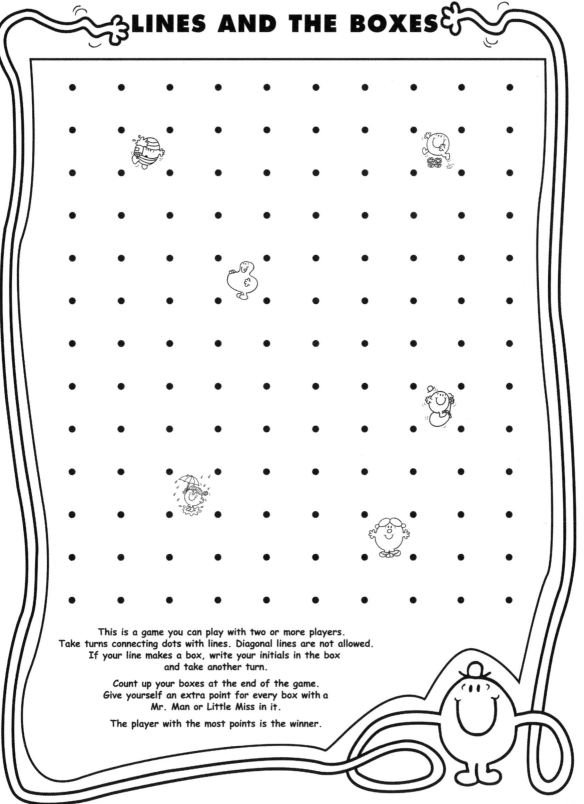

This is a game you can play with two or more players.
Take turns connecting dots with lines. Diagonal lines are not allowed.
If your line makes a box, write your initials in the box
and take another turn.

Count up your boxes at the end of the game.
Give yourself an extra point for every box with a
Mr. Man or Little Miss in it.

The player with the most points is the winner.

FIND THE DIFFERENCES

Can you find 20 differences
between these two pictures?

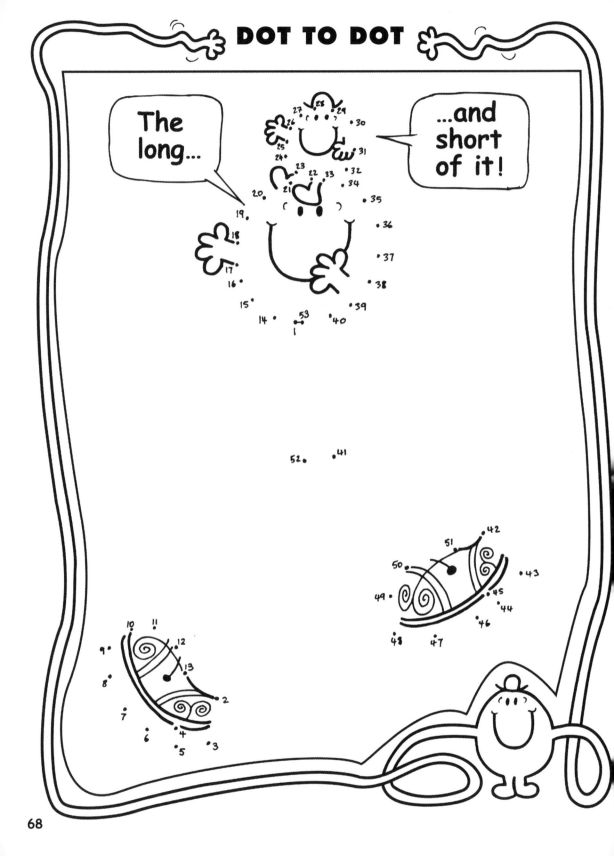

COLORING FUN

Color Little Miss Ditzy's hair yellow.

Color Little Miss Fickle's hat pink. What color are her bows?

Put red polka dots on Little Miss Splendid's hat.

Color Little Miss Wise pink. Write a message on her flag.

Little Miss Bossy has a red hat with a yellow band. Color it.

Little Miss Magic has red shoes. Draw green stripes on her bow.

Little Miss Scatterbrain is red. She wears blue gloves. Color her.

Color Little Miss Somersault's hair yellow. Color her body blue.

Color Little Miss Quick's ribbon. It's blue. Her shoes and hair are brown.

Color Little Miss Lucky's nose blue.

Unscramble the names of these
Mr. Men and Little Misses.

MR. MUCLSY _ _ _ _ _ _

MR. PYMURG _ _ _ _ _ _

LITTLE MISS SNNIESHU _ _ _ _ _ _ _ _

LITTLE MISS LDPISDNE _ _ _ _ _ _ _ _

MR. SWON _ _ _ _

LITTLE MISS YTIZD _ _ _ _ _

70

COLOR-BY-NUMBERS

Little Miss Trouble has to write on the blackboard.

Use the guide to color the picture.

1=Green, 2=Yellow, 3=Red, 4=Brown, 5=Black, 6=Blue

Mr. Impossible can fly!
Which flower did he fly from?

A   B   C   D   E   F

Color the correct flower.

Little Miss Shy is at the beach.
Use the grid to help you complete
the picture, then color it.

Come out, Mr. Daydream!
I know you're in
there somewhere!

Color all the dotted
areas blue.

Toss a coin.
Heads, you color in all the hats.
Tails, you color in all the shoes!

WORD SEARCH

Search for the Mr. Men and Little Misses hidden below.
Look up, down, across, backward, and diagonally.

Happy   Naughty   Muddle   Topsy-Turvy
Nosey   Tickle   Greedy   Clever   Small   Bossy
Fussy   Quiet   Bad   Bump   Chatterbox

```
C H A T T E R B O X N E R A H
D T G B R A A U O W A O T A A
Y S S U F Q U M A S P A S R P
W Q A F D S A P I O S S D E P
E Z T O P S Y T U R V Y A V Y
A X C V A N A L K J H G F E P
R I O P M A M U D D L E A L O
T Y T H G U A N I U Y T R C I
Y I N G H J K L M N A T R A A
U A A T Z X X C V B I W E K L
Y D E E R G Q A G C S M A L L
M A M I Z S F H K
N B F U X D A L
B A V Q C A E A
```

MATCHING

Match each Little Miss to her shadow.

COLOR-BY-NUMBERS

Mr. Bump is having trouble
washing his windows.
Use the guide to color the picture.

1=Blue, 2=Yellow, 3=Brown,
4=Red, 5=Gray, 6=Black, 7=Green

COLORING FUN

FIND THE DIFFERENCES

Mr. Grumpy's all wet!

Can you spot the 10 differences between these two pictures?

How many sneezes do your eyes see?

Mr. Stingy has forgotten where he buried his money. Can you help him find it?

DOT TO DOT

TANGLED UP

Who is Little Miss Greedy
lunching with today?

Follow the line to see.

Mr. Nonsense

Little Miss Quick

Mr. Perfect

Little Miss Late

Mr. Strong

Little Miss Tiny loves her new toy.
Do you know what she named it?
Use the secret code to find out.

$$\overline{13}\ \overline{18}\ .\quad \overline{2}\ \overline{5}\ \overline{1}\ \overline{18}$$

1	2	3	4	5	6	7	8	9	10	11	12	13
A	B	C	D	E	F	G	H	I	J	K	L	M

14	15	16	17	18	19	20	21	22	23	24	25	26
N	O	P	Q	R	S	T	U	V	W	X	Y	Z

The Code

COLORING FUN

ODD ONE OUT

Which Mr. Funny is the odd one out?

MISSING PIECES

Mr. Bump has bumped his head again! Match each square to the hole in the picture and draw it in.

A-MAZING!

Help Mr. Dizzy
find his way home.

COLORING FUN

103

BRAINTEASER

Some Mr. Men and Little Misses are spending the afternoon in the country. Others are spending the day in the city. Color in the friends who are in the country. Circle the ones who are in the city.

Mr. Nosey

Little Miss Chatterbox

Little Miss Bossy

Little Miss Splendid

Mr. Bump

COLOR-BY-NUMBERS

The sun is shining on a happy day.
Use the guide to color the picture.

1=Green, 2=Yellow, 3=Red,
4=Brown, 5=Purple, 6=Blue

What a silly bath!

Which tap should Mr. Silly turn on to fill his bath?

COLORING FUN

MATCHING

Mr. Greedy has dropped all his cakes.
That will teach him to be so greedy!
Match the cakes to their shadows.

DOT TO DOT

Mr. Impossible

STORY TIME

One day, Mr. Uppity and Little Miss Bossy were

at the _____ , eating _____ .
　　　　　　　　a place　　　　　　　　　　　　a type of food

All of a sudden, a/an _____ bit
　　　　　　　　　　　an animal

Mr. Uppity right on the _____ !
　　　　　　　　　　　　a part of the body

"Watch out!" Little Miss Bossy said.

"Give him your _____ so that he'll stop
　　　　　　　a type of food

_____ your _____ ."
an action ending in "ing"　　a part of the body

Mr. Uppity threw a/an _____
　　　　　　　　　　　　an object

at the _____ . "Wow!" he said.
　　　　an animal

"I didn't know I was so _____ !"
　　　　　　　　　　　adjective

COLOR-BY-NUMBERS

Little Miss Naughty is up to her tricks again! Color in the scene using the color guide below.

1=Purple, 2=Yellow, 3=Brown, 4=Red, 5=Blue, 6=Green

FIND THE DIFFERENCES

Water fight!

Can you spot the 10 differences between these two pictures?

COUNTING FUN

Mr. Men and Little Misses are lining up to watch the game tonight. Count them all. How many Mr. Men and Little Misses are there?

MATCHING

Match each Mr. Man to his shadow.

A-MAZING!

Mr. Forgetful has lost his hat. Can you help him remember where he left it?

COMPLETE THE PICTURE

It's another happy day for Mr. Happy. Make the day even better by completing the picture. Use the grid to help you.

ODD ONE OUT

Little Miss Somersault is practicing for her gymnastics competition. Find the one that is different from the rest and color it.

Mr. Snow

Activity Answer Key

p.44 A-MAZING!
Mr. Worry

p.45 FIND THE DIFFERENCES
Missing tree;
Mr. Strong's hat;
Mr. Strong's mouth;
Mr. Tickle's glove;
string on sled;
lace on Little Miss Sunshine's skate;
pompom on Little Miss Sunshine's hat;
snow under Mr. Tickle's left hand;
snow on top of right mountain;
snow next to sled

p.48 TANGLED UP
Mr. Uppity

p.49 SECRET CODE
Mr. Nervous is hiding because Mr. Noisy shouts too much.

p.51 MISSING PIECES
1 = A;
2 = C;
3 = B

p.54 MATCHING
J

p.58 A-MAZING!
Mr. Slow and Mr. Silly

p.60 ODD ONE OUT
E

p.61 TANGLED UP
Mr. Small

p.64 A-MAZING!

p.67 FIND THE DIFFERENCES
Fruit on the tree;
sheep; cloud;
ray on sun;
bushes on hill;
line in Little Miss Sunshine's hair;
Little Miss Sunshine's eyes;
bushes in front of Little Miss Sunshine;
flower next to road;
lines after puffs of smoke;
swirl on back of car;
flower stem in Mr. Funny's hat;
squiggle by Mr. Funny's eye;
Mr. Funny's glove;
Mr. Funny's fingers on steering wheel;
spoke on steering wheel;
dot on hood;
circle on front tire; Mr. Small's glove;
Mr. Small's hat

p.70 SCRAMBLED UP
Mr. Clumsy;
Mr. Grumpy;
Little Miss Sunshine;
Little Miss Splendid;
Mr. Snow;
Little Miss Ditzy

Activity Answer Key

p.74 TANGLED UP
D

p.75 A-MAZING!

p.81 WORD SEARCH

p.84 MATCHING
1 = D;
2 = C;
3 = A;
4 = B

p.85 TANGLED UP
Mr. Happy

p.88 FIND THE DIFFERENCES
Sun;
line on beach ball;
cloud;
Little Miss Sunshine's eye;
Little Miss Sunshine's pigtail;
lines in Little Miss Sunshine's hair;
Mr. Happy's smile; Mr. Happy's foot;
Mr. Grumpy's hat;
splash near Mr. Grumpy

p.89 COUNTING FUN
Seventeen

p.90 A-MAZING!

p.95 TANGLED UP
Mr. Strong

p.96 SECRET CODE
Mr. Bear

p.98 ODD ONE OUT
A

p.99 MISSING PIECES
1 = C;
2 = A;
3 = B

p.101 A-MAZING!

p.104 BRAINTEASER
Country:
Little Miss Bossy,
Mr. Bump,
Little Miss Tiny
City:
Little Miss Chatterbox,
Mr. Nosey,
Little Miss Splendid

Activity Answer Key

p.106 TANGLED UP
B

p.108 MATCHING
1 = B;
2 = C;
3 = D;
4 = E;
5 = A

p.111 HOW MUCH?
$91.00

p.115 FIND THE DIFFERENCES
Petals on flower in Mr. Funny's hat;
tube from Mr. Funny's hat;
Mr. Funny's eyes;
water on Little Miss Wise's umbrella;
balloon on Mr. Greedy;
Little Miss Fun's balloon;
Little Miss Wise's thumb;
lace on Mr. Funny's shoe;
Mr. Greedy's smile;
Little Miss Fun's bow

p.116 COUNTING FUN
Sixteen

p.118 BANDAGE BANDIT
Mr. Nosey

p.119 MATCHING
1 = D;
2 = C;
3 = A;
4 = B

p.120 A-MAZING!

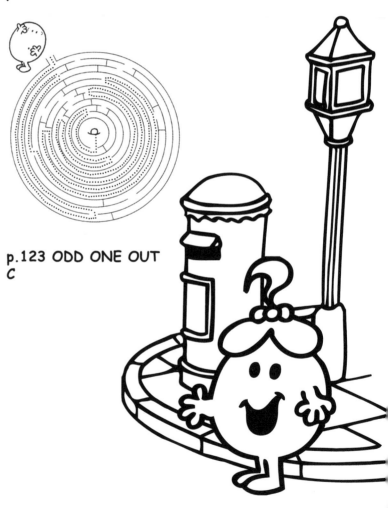

p.123 ODD ONE OUT
C

Mr. Happy's Birthday

I am always happy. Especially on my birthday.
Just look what my friends gave me!
Connect the dots to find out what my presents are.

But, oh dear! I floated up into a maze of fluffy clouds.
"Come back down," called out Mr. Bump.
Can you show me the way to the ground?

131

Then all the balloon strings got tangled up.
"I'll just keep the red balloon," I said.
Which string goes to the red balloon?

132

Mr. Tickle said we were going to Mr. Messy's house.
We lost our way. Can you find the path to his house?

Now I know why he is called Mr. Messy!
Just look at his house. You can make a messy picture, too.
Color the bottom picture the same as the top one.

We went out into the woods.
"Let's play hide and seek," said Mr. Messy.
"Let's look for Mr. Bump, Mr. Tickle, and Mr. Nosey."

"Your present is over there," said Mr. Bump.
Which long, twisting path should I follow?

"We've got a birthday present for you," said Mr. Nosey.
"But first, you have to draw what you think it will be."
What did I draw? Connect the dots and you'll see!

"Happy birthday, Mr. Happy!" said Mr. Greedy.
"Here's your present." It was a birthday cake.
What a party we all had!

Alphabet and Counting Fun!

This is Mr. Bump.
He is starting to read.

Draw lines to match the things that are the same.

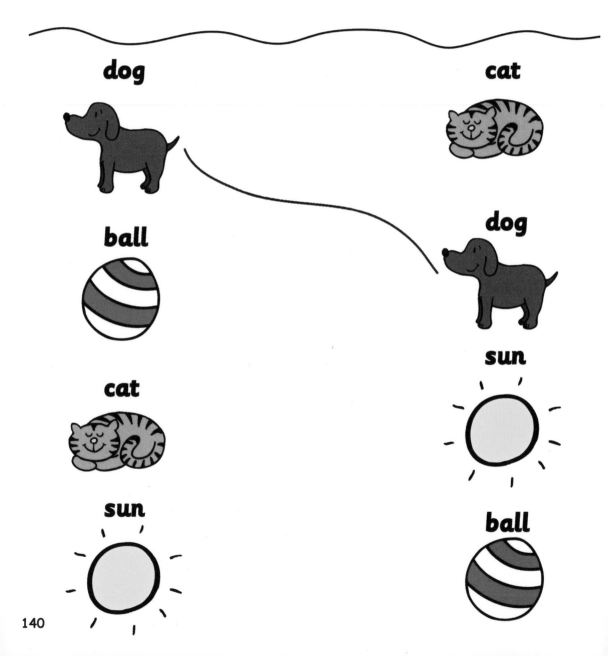

dog

cat

ball

dog

cat

sun

sun

ball

Help Mr. Bump to find the odd one out.

Draw a circle around the odd one out in each row.

bee				
hat				
bag				
key				

This is Little Miss Sunshine.
She knows the letters in her name.

Draw lines to match the letters that
are the same. The first one is done for you.

s - u - n - s - h - i - n - e

s

n

s

h

n

i

u

e

Write her name here: S _ _ _ _ _ _ _

Little Miss Sunshine is flying her kite.

Find the objects below in the
picture and color them in.
Copy the words.

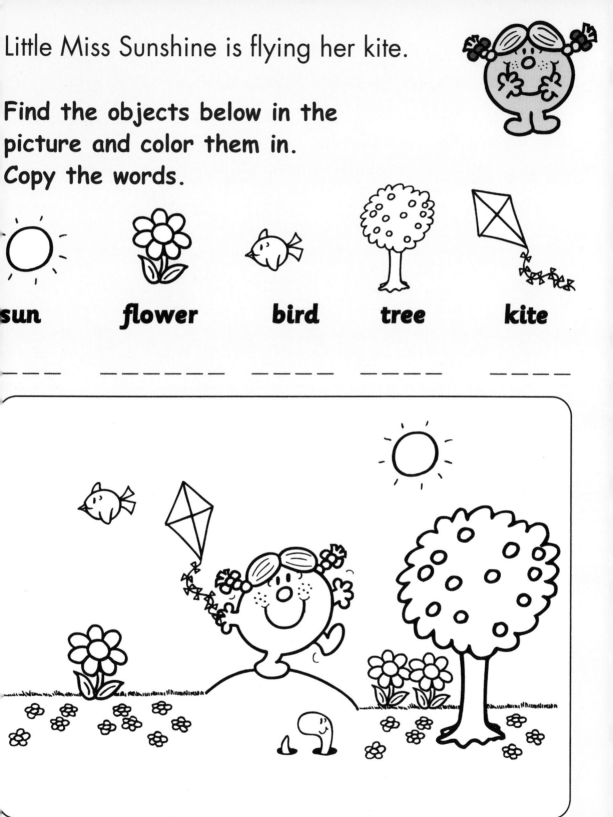

sun   *flower*   **bird**   **tree**   **kite**

This is Mr. Noisy.
When he sings, his mouth makes
the same shape as a letter O

Draw a circle around each letter O.

o

o

e

e

e

e

e

o

e

o

o

How many did you find?

Mr. Noisy is looking for some letters.

Look at the beginning sound of each picture. Circle the letters that are the same.

a   a   c   **a**   e   **a**   o

apple

   e   o   a   o   e   o

orange

   a   c   o   c   c   a

cat

   c   s   a   s   s   o

sun

   n   i   u   a   u   u

umbrella

This is Little Miss Splendid. She has drawn this picture for you to color. The letters tell you which colors to use.

g=green, b=blue, r=red, y=yellow, o=orange,
Color all the apples red.

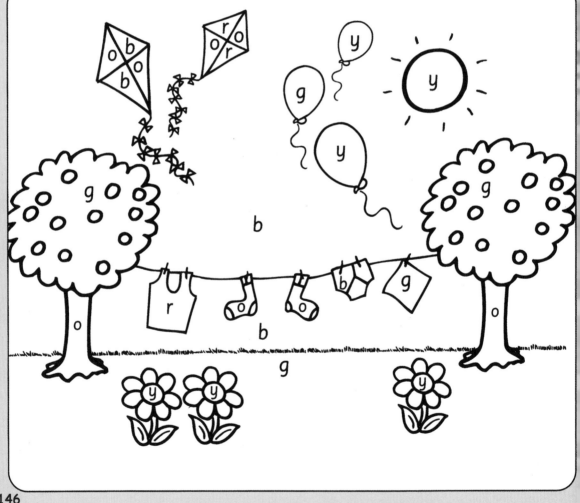

Here are some words to match.
Draw 3 lines between 3 words
that are the same.
The first one is done for you.

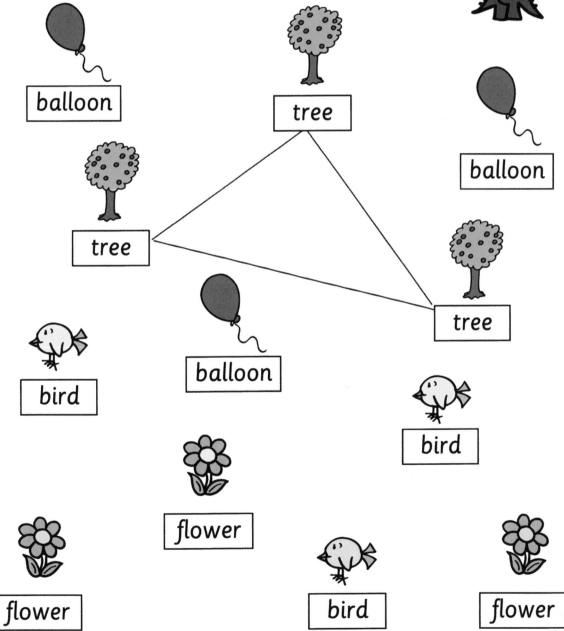

balloon

tree

balloon

tree

tree

bird

balloon

bird

flower

flower

bird

flower

This is Mr. Tall.
He is as tall as a very tall tree!

Draw a circle around each letter _t_.

tree

How many did you find?

148

Draw a circle around the odd one out in each row.

able

iger

ent

eapot

149

This is Little Miss Busy.
She is busy reading.

Help her match each picture to
its correct letter sound.

f *is for*

s *is for*

h *is for*

t *is for*

<u>s</u>un

<u>h</u>at

<u>t</u>ent

<u>f</u>ox

Little Miss Busy is in the park.

Find the objects below in the picture and color them in.

1 sun   **2** trees   **3** balls   **4** hats   **5** flowers

This is Mr. Tickle.
He is reaching for the letters
on the shelves.

Draw a circle around the odd one
out on each shelf.

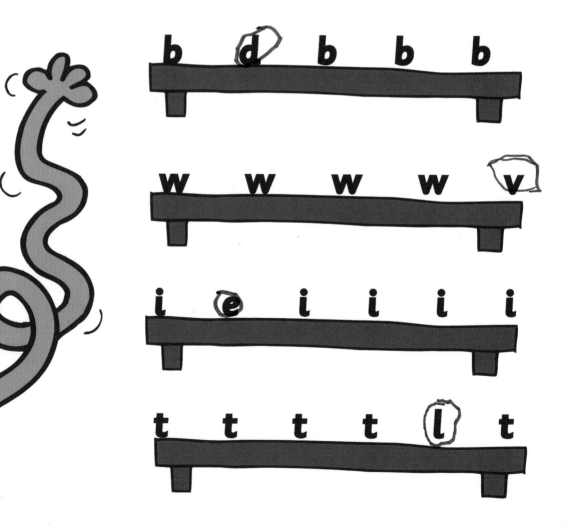

b   d   b   b   b

w   w   w   w   v

i   e   i   i   i   i

t   t   t   t   l   t

Help Mr. Tickle match each picture to its correct letter sound.

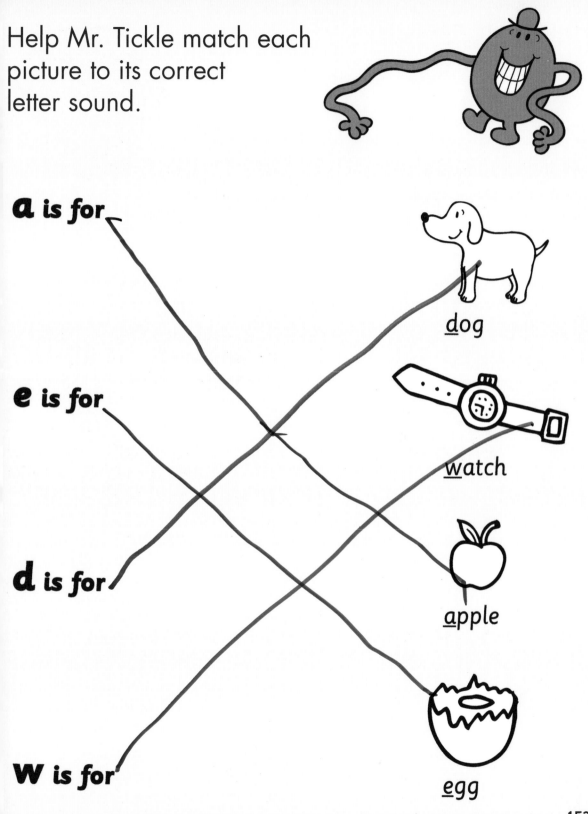

a is for

e is for

d is for

w is for

<u>d</u>og

<u>w</u>atch

<u>a</u>pple

<u>e</u>gg

This is Little Miss Helpful.
She likes to help, but sometimes
she's not helpful at all.
Look what happened when
she did some painting.
Tell the story from the pictures.
Then draw what you think happens next.

154

Little Miss Helpful is looking at these pictures.

Help her to join the pictures which begin with the same sound.

This is Mr. Small.
He is on vacation.
Color the picture.
The letters tell you which colors to use.

g=green, r=red, y=yellow, b=blue

Look at the word on the left.
Then find the word that is the
same along the line.
Draw a circle around it.

fish	*frog*	*fish*	*four*	*flower*
sock	**sail**	**soap**	**sock**	**seal**
watch	**worm**	**wall**	**watch**	**wheel**
boat	**boat**	**bird**	**belt**	**bags**

This is Little Miss Tiny.
She's learning about letter sounds.
You can, too.

Match each picture to its correct letter sound.

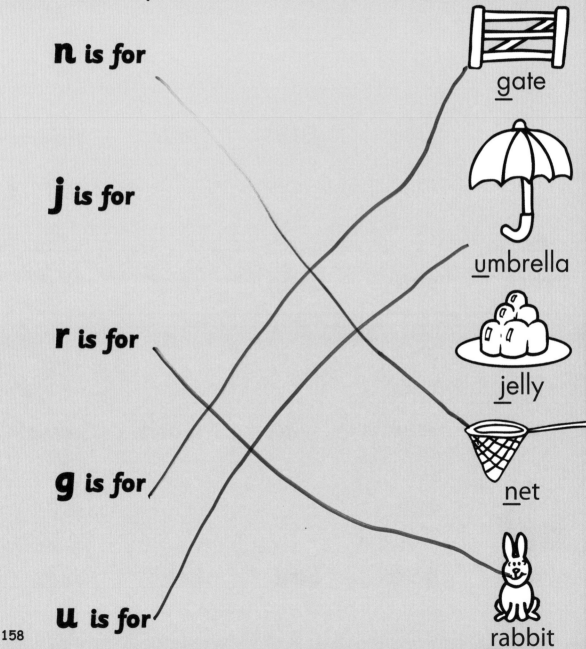

n is for

j is for

r is for

g is for

u is for

gate

umbrella

jelly

net

rabbit

Little Miss Tiny is a as tiny as a mouse.

Find the tiny letters in the picture
and circle them.

How many did you find?

This is Mr. Nosey.
He wants to find the way to
Mr. Messy's house.

Join the letters of the alphabet in
order to find the correct path through the trees.

a b c d e f g h i j k l m

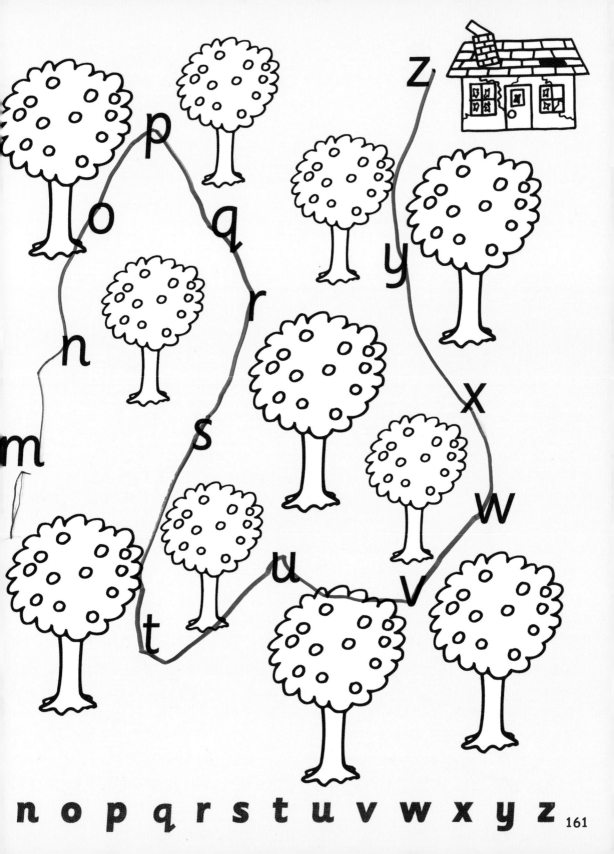

z p o q y n m s r x t u w v

n o p q r s t u v w x y z 161

This is Mr. Greedy.
There is only **1** Mr. Greedy.
Write **1**.

Here is Mr. Greedy with his friends.
Draw a circle around him and color him in.

Match the pictures that are the same.

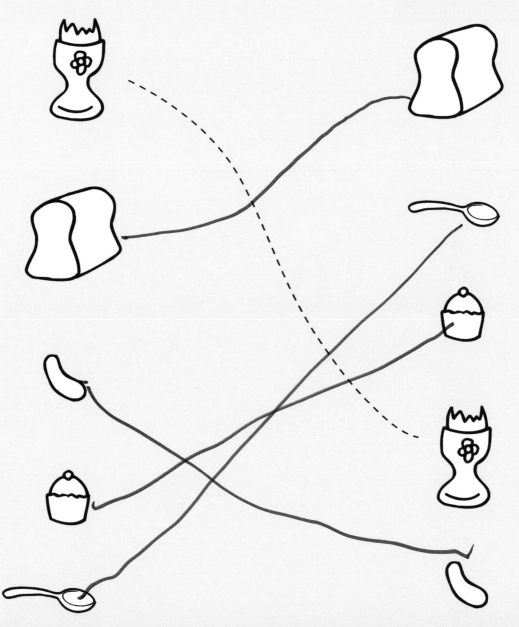

163

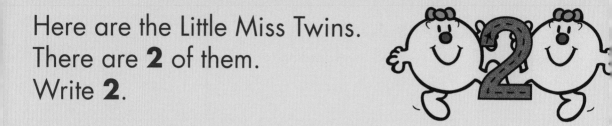

Here are the Little Miss Twins.
There are **2** of them.
Write **2**.

Find 2 things that are the same in each line.
Then color them in.

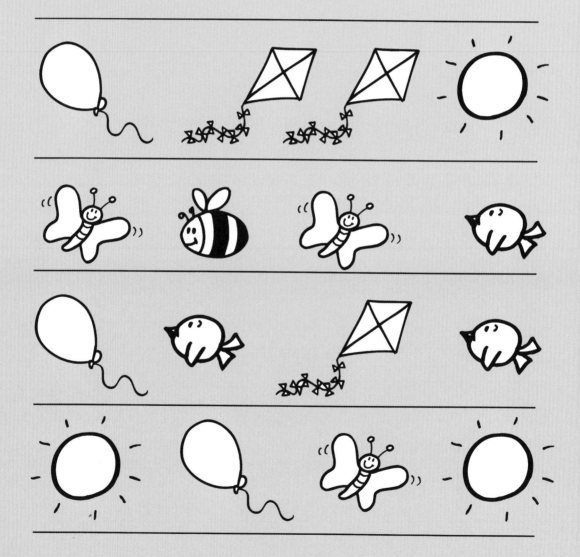

Connect the dots to finish the pictures. How many fish can you count?

Color them in.

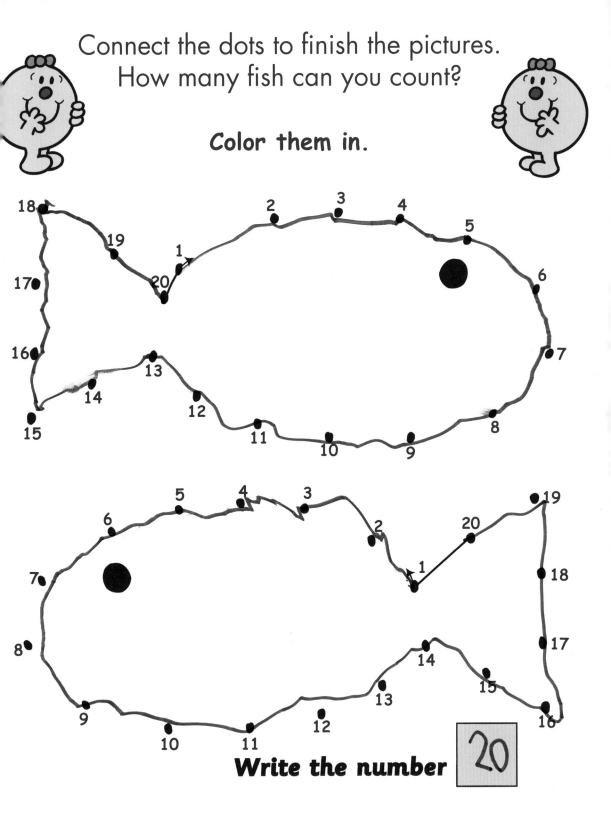

Write the number 20

This is Mr. Chatterbox.
He can count to **3**.
Write **3**.

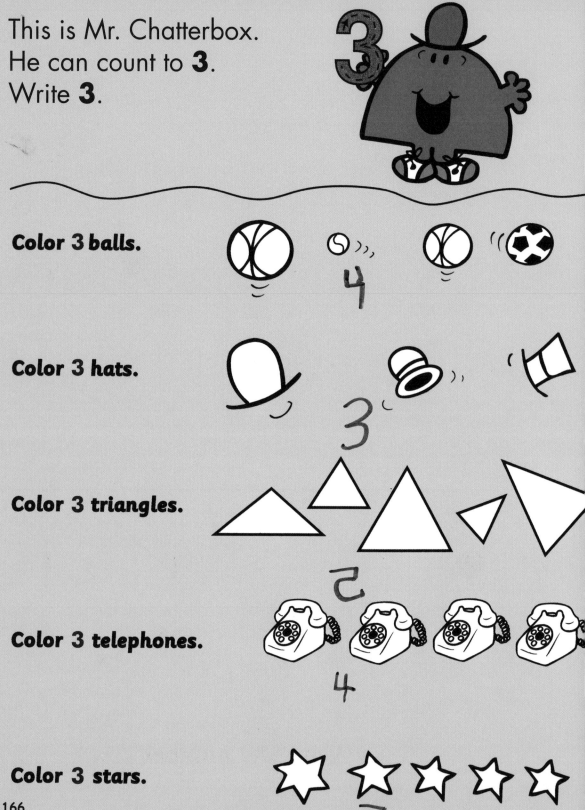

Color 3 balls.

Color 3 hats.

Color 3 triangles.

Color 3 telephones.

Color 3 stars.

Color the balloons using 3 colors.
1=red

2=blue

3=green

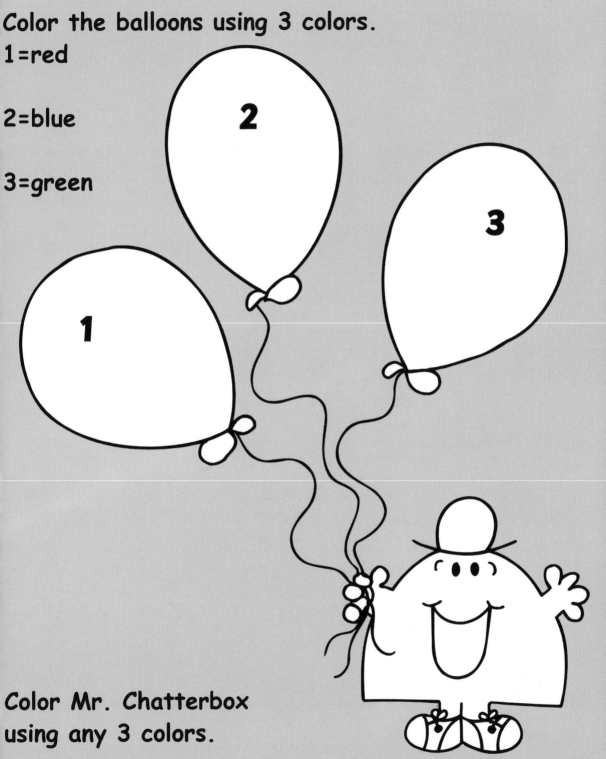

Color Mr. Chatterbox
using any 3 colors.

This is Little Miss Naughty.
She is holding the number **4**.
Write **4**.

Color the flowers that have 4 petals.

Little Miss Naughty likes
to paint.
Here are her pictures.

Count the things in the boxes
and match them to the correct number.

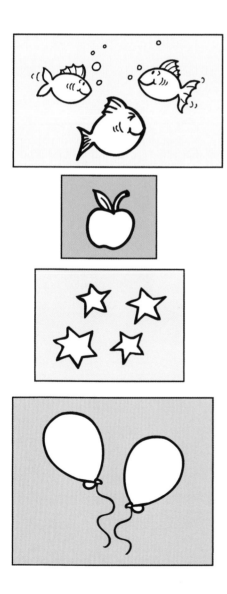

1 apple

2 balloons

3 fish

4 stars

This is Mr. Happy.
Mr. Happy's favorite number is **5**.
Write **5**.

Color 5 circles blue .
Color 5 circles red .
Color 5 circles yellow .
Color 5 circles green .
Color 5 circles brown .

Finish each line with the correct
number of pictures.

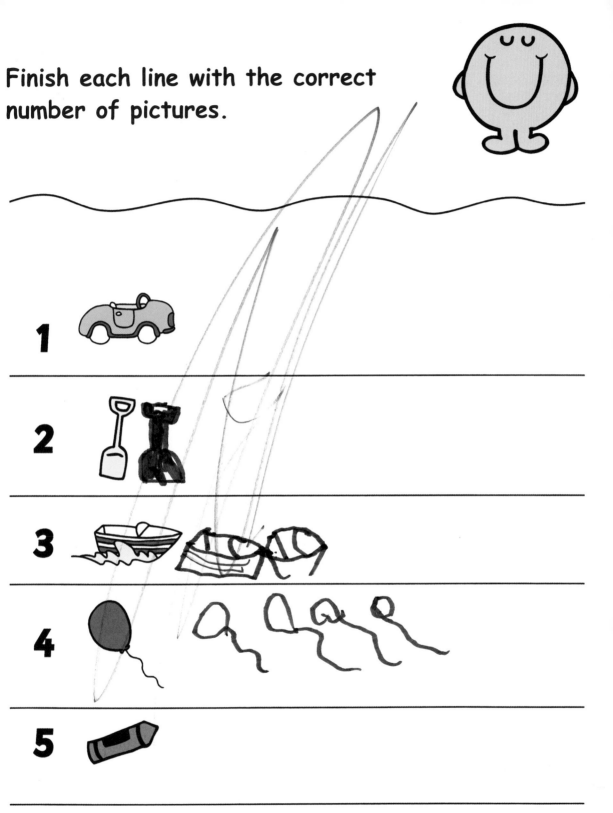

1

2

3

4

5

This is Little Miss Sunshine.
She can count to **6**.
Write **6**.

Draw some more hearts so that there are 6. Color them.

Draw some more buttons so that there are 6. Color them.

Draw some more squares so that there are 6. Color them.

Draw some more ladybugs so that there are 6. Color them.

Look at the top picture.
Then look at the bottom picture.

Find 6 things that are missing in
the bottom picture.

Draw them.

This is Mr. Nosey.
He is holding the number **7**.
Write **7**.

Count the keyholes, then draw one more.

How many are there now?

Show Mr. Nosey the way along the road.

Count the numbers and join the lines.

Color 7 flowers.

This is Little Miss Tiny.
She is counting things that rhyme.
Write **8**.

Draw some more peas so that there are **8**.

Draw some more bees so that there are **8**.

Draw some more trees so that there are **8**.

Draw some more keys so that there are **8**.

Which box has 8 balls?

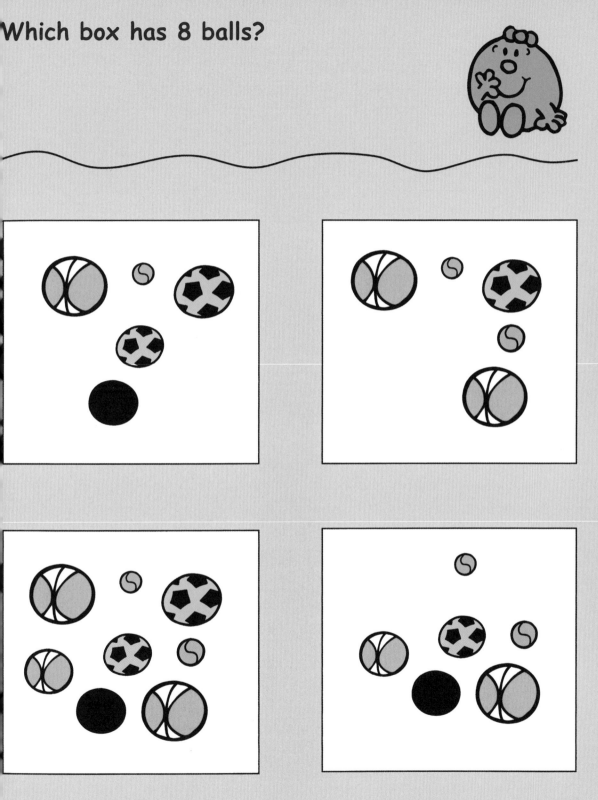

This is Mr. Grumpy.
There are **9** raindrops falling onto
his umbrella.
Write **9**.

Color in 9 raindrops.

Look at the numbers on
Mr. Grumpy's hat.

Draw a circle around every number 9 that you
can see.

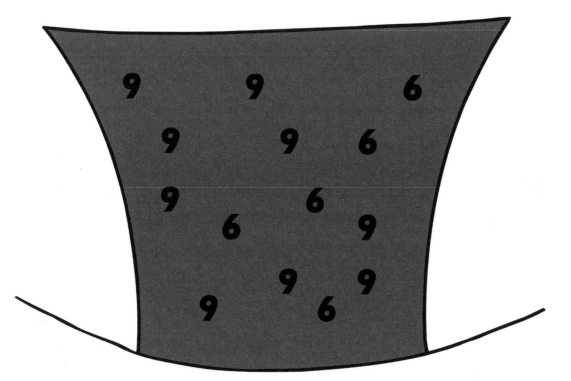

Count them and write the number.

This is Little Miss Magic.
She loves the number **10**.
Write **10**.

Connect the numbers in the right order.

1

2

3

5

6

4

7

8

9

10

Little Miss Magic has made 10 wands appear.

Can you find them all?

Circle them.

Here is Mr. Greedy again.

It's lunchtime.

He's having pizza.

Number each slice.
How many slices altogether?

A Day with Mr. Messy

I'm the messiest person I know.
Look what happened when I tried to tidy my bedroom.
Have you ever seen such a mess?

Mr. Happy said his garden needed to be tidied.
Do you think that was a good idea? Look where I put
all the leaves! Connect the dots to find out.

Then I bumped into Mr. Bump. Well, he bumped into me.
He was looking for someone.
Who do you think it was?

Mr. Nosey, Mr. Bump, and I walked off along a winding path.
We were going to visit Mr. Tickle.
Which path took us to Mr. Tickle's house?

Mr. Tickle lived in a very tidy sort of a house.
After I'd been there a while, things looked very different.
Connect the dots and you'll see why!

Mr. Tickle didn't think that was very funny at all!
In fact, he tried to make me tidy everything up.
I ran off to find Mr. Greedy. Which way did I go?

Mr. Greedy was having a picnic. All to himself.
Just look at all the ice cream. What flavors were they?
You can decide when you color them in.

When I got home, Mr. Happy had played a trick on me.
He had tidied up my bedroom! I untidied it right away!
Use the same colors to finish the picture underneath.

In the morning, I found Mr. Bump knocking things over in my garden. What a mess. It looked lovely!

Doodle Fun

DOODLE FUN

Mr. Birthday always knows exactly what to get his friends for their birthdays. What would Mr. Birthday get you for your birthday?

Ouch! Mr. Bump can't stop bumping into things!
What knocked him over this time?

197

DOODLE FUN

The Mr. Men and Little Misses love to read!
Design a cover for your favorite book.

Mr. Greedy

Mr. Chatterbox

Little Miss Fickle

Little Miss Busy

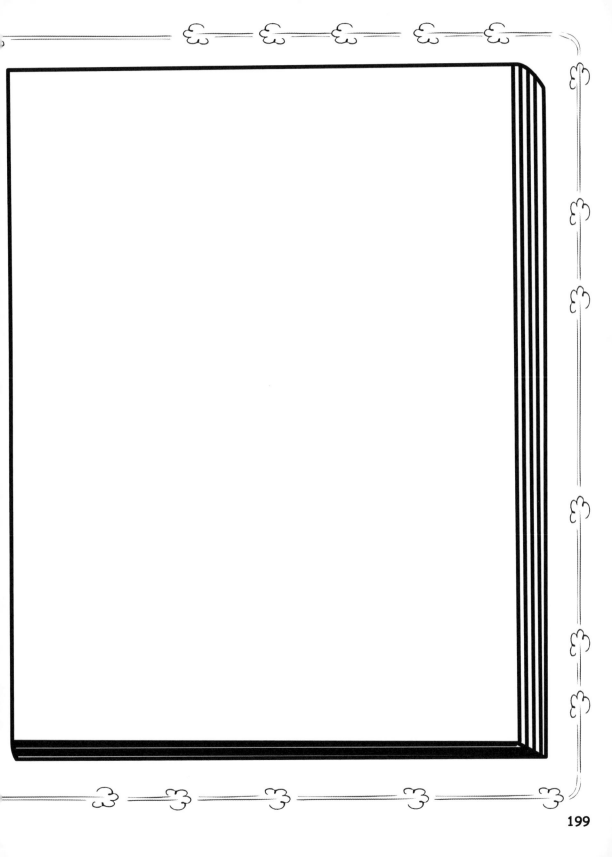

DOODLE FUN

Adventure is always nearby when Mr. Cool is around!
Draw what adventures you would have together.

201

Little Miss Chatterbox loves to talk and talk and talk and talk . . . Who is she talking to? Draw her friend on the other end of the line.

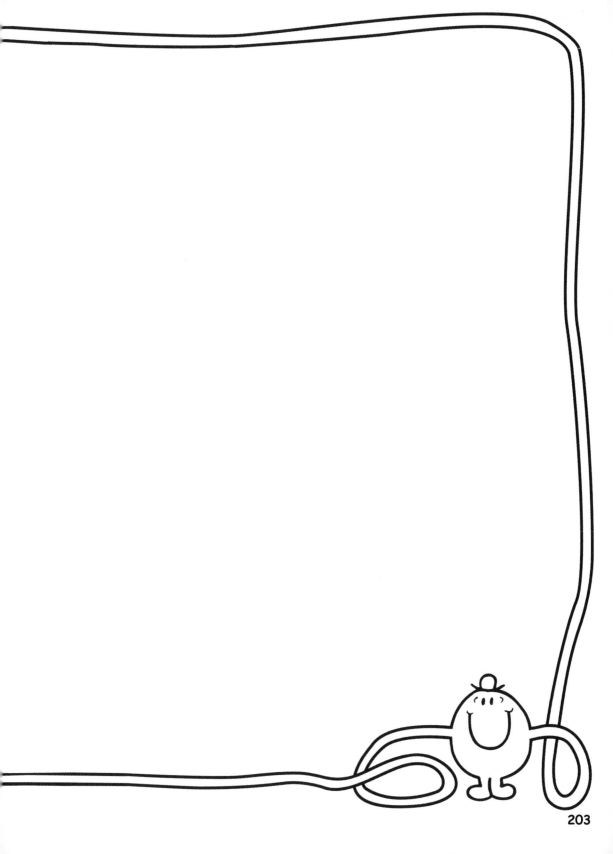

203

DOODLE FUN

It's a dance party! Draw a disco ball and some more dancers to really get it going!

DOODLE FUN

Splash! Mr. Messy is painting a mural, and he's getting paint everywhere! Draw what he is painting using at least five different colors.

DOODLE FUN

There are lots of animals in Mr. Men Land.
What other animals do you think live there?

La la la! Mr. Noisy loves to sing!
What song is he singing? Write out the lyrics to
the song, or draw the story the song is about.

DOODLE FUN

The Little Misses are starting a band!
Give them each an instrument to play.
Which Little Miss would be the best singer?

Little Miss Shy

Little Miss Scary

Little Miss Twins

DOODLE FUN

Mr. Funny tells the funniest jokes in Mr. Men Land!
What are your favorite jokes?

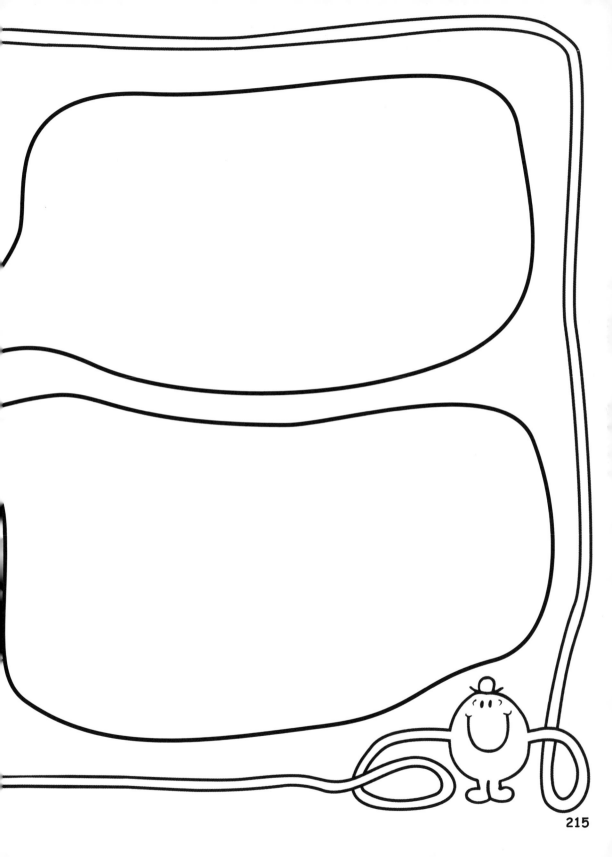

215

DOODLE FUN

Abracadabra! Little Miss Magic is casting
a spell to make her favorite animal appear!
Draw which animal it is. What other magic
can Little Miss Magic do with her wand?

217

DOODLE FUN

Mr. Greedy loves to eat. Draw a feast for him with all of your favorite foods. And don't forget dessert!

Mr. Tickle's loooooooong arms just can't stop tickling! Draw someone for him to tickle.

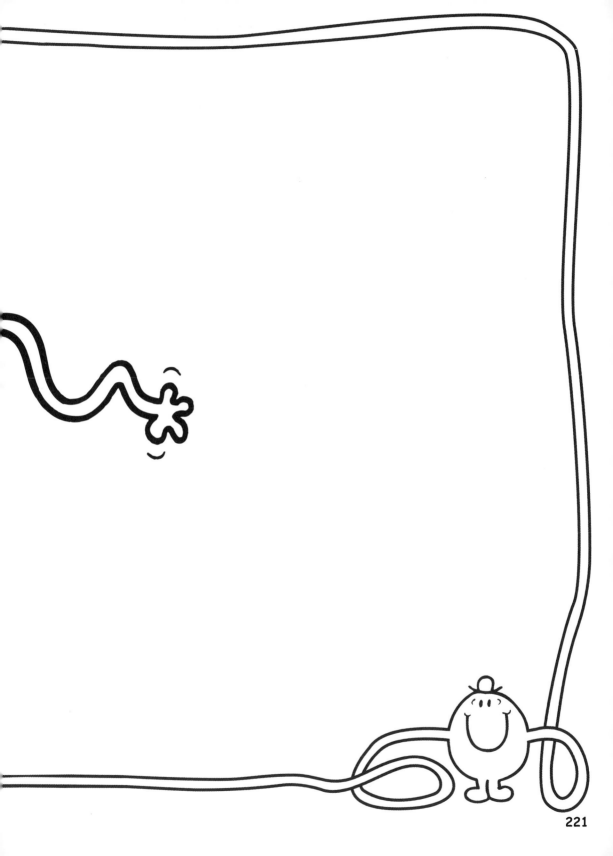

DOODLE FUN

Little Miss Whoops is getting ready for teatime.
Whoops! What kinds of food would you prepare
for teatime? And who would you invite?

DOODLE FUN

Mr. Greedy, Mr. Tickle, Mr. Happy, and Mr. Small
are going to a birthday party! But whose is it?
Draw whose birthday it is, and add a cake, gifts,
and anything else they need for the party!

DOODLE FUN

Uh-oh! Little Miss Naughty has covered Little Miss Splendid, Little Miss Bossy, and Little Miss Star in paint! Add splashes of paint to the three Little Misses. How many colors did Little Miss Naughty use?

DOODLE FUN

The Little Misses' favorite celebrity has just landed in Mr. Men Land! Draw your favorite celebrity getting out of the airplane.

DOODLE FUN

Little Miss Splendid is playing dress-up!
She makes a great princess. Give the
other Little Misses costumes, too.

Little Miss Splendid

Little Miss Trouble

Little Miss Brainy

Little Miss Quick

Little Miss Late

Little Miss Shy

DOODLE FUN

Zzzzzzzzzzzzzz . . . Mr. Greedy, Mr. Quiet,
and Mr. Stingy are fast asleep.
What are they dreaming about?

DOODLE FUN

Mr. Strong is the strongest person in Mr. Men Land!
Draw a really heavy item in his hands.
Don't worry, he can handle it!

DOODLE FUN

Mr. Grumpy is shopping at the grocery store.
Give him a cart to hold all his food!
What other kinds of food does he need to buy?

DOODLE FUN

Parties are Little Miss Fun's very favorite things! Help her decorate for her next bash. What kind of party is it?

DOODLE FUN

Little Miss Somersault is full of energy!
Draw an obstacle course with things for her
to climb up, jump over, and crawl under.

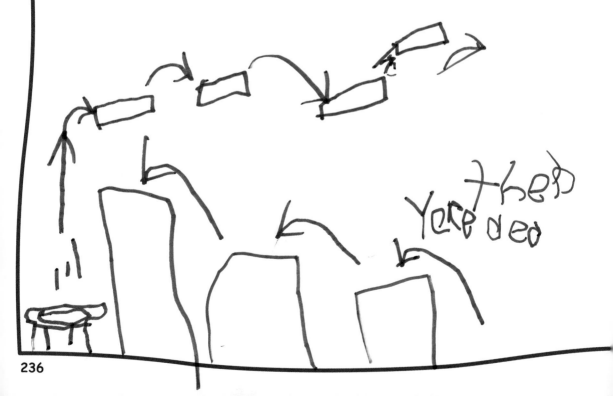

DOODLE FUN

Little Miss Greedy and Mr. Forgetful are on their
way to the park! Finish drawing their cars.
What are they driving past?

239

DOODLE FUN

Little Miss Splendid is shopping for the most splendid hat in town! Draw a lot of interesting hats for her to try on.

DOODLE FUN

Splashing in puddles in the rain is fun—but wet!
Give Little Miss Naughty rain boots and a raincoat.
Who else is playing in the rain?

Little Miss Sunshine

Mr. Worry

DOODLE FUN

Everyone in Mr. Men Land lives in a house that fits their personality. What does your dream house look like?

Mr. Funny

Little Miss Somersault

Little Miss Curious

Mr. Perfect

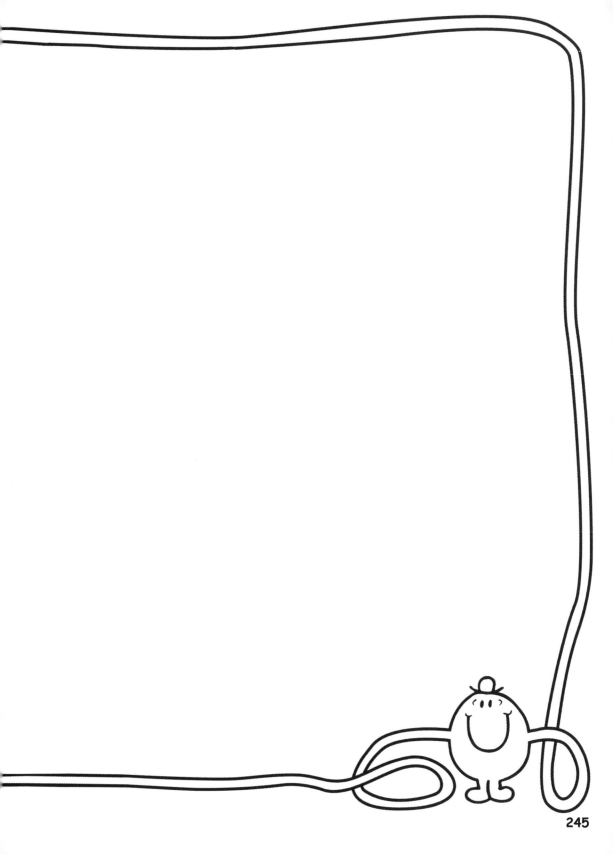

245

Mr. Impossible can do all kinds of impossible things—like fly! What impossible things do you wish you could do?

DOODLE FUN

Little Miss Princess is in her castle looking out over Mr. Men Land. What does she see? Whose houses can she see from her window?

DOODLE FUN

Mr. Fussy loves to garden. Fill his garden with flowers!
What else do you find in a garden?

DOODLE FUN

Mr. Busy always has something to do.
Where is he on his way to right now?
Draw a faster way for him to get there!

DOODLE FUN

Ta-da! Little Miss Star is putting on a play for her friends.
Draw the background and the props for her show.
What is her play about?

DOODLE FUN

Mr. Happy and Little Miss Sunshine can always find a reason to smile! What things make you happy?

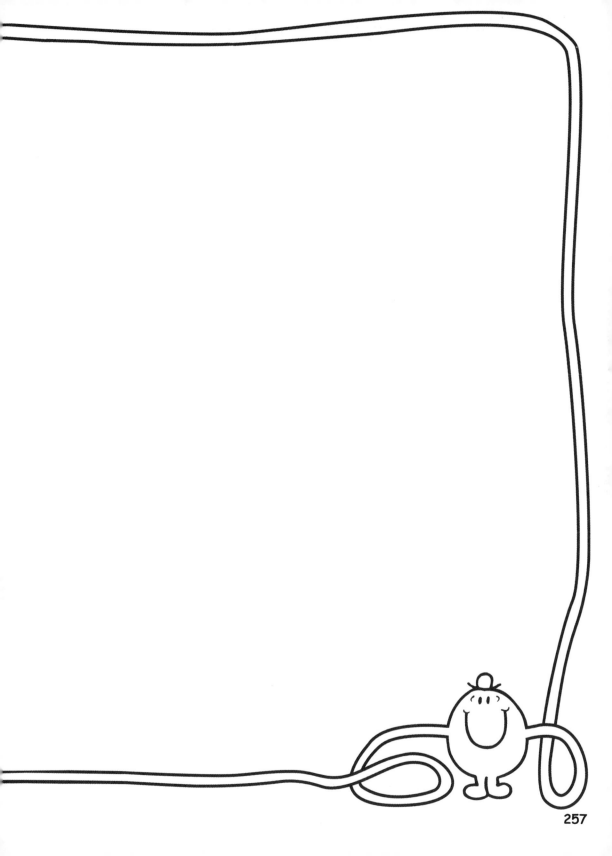

257

DOODLE FUN

Mr. Small is writing a story—if he can manage
to lift the pencil! What is his story about?
Draw pictures to go with his writing.

DOODLE FUN

Mr. Uppity is one of the richest people in the world. Draw a big mansion for him. What other kinds of things would he own?

DOODLE FUN

All the Mr. Men and Little Misses have
big personalities! Which one is most like you?
What would you look like if you lived in Mr. Men Land?

Mr. Bounce

Mr. Happy

Mr. Bump

Mr. Mischief

Mr. Quiet

Little Miss Fun

Little Miss Neat

Mr. Noisy

Mr. Strong

Mr. Greedy

Little Miss Helpful

Little Miss Naughty

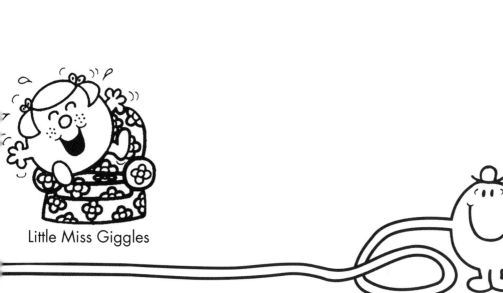

Little Miss Giggles

Splat! Mr. Happy and Mr. Nosey are having a snowball fight! Who else is joining the game?

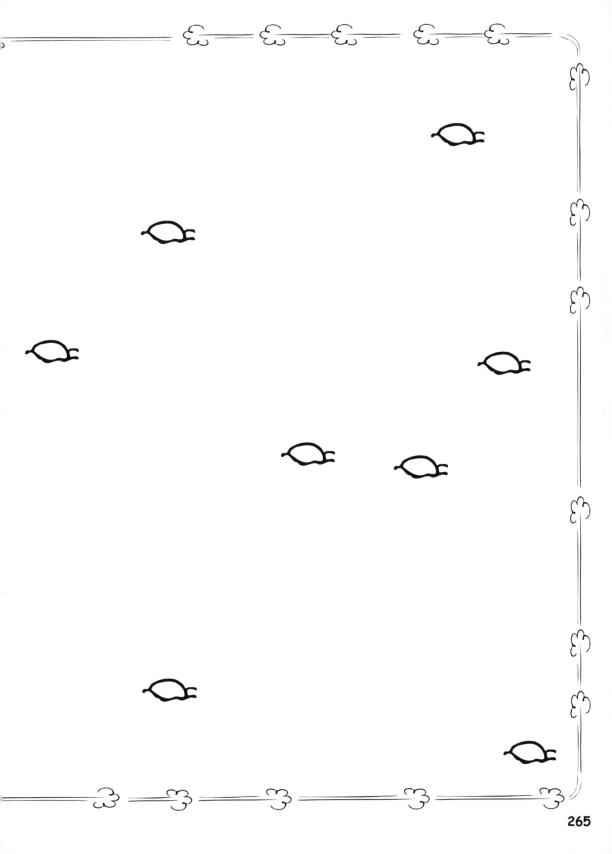

DOODLE FUN

The Mr. Men and Little Misses love to play in the snow!
What do you like to do in the snow?
Add more friends to join the fun!

DOODLE FUN

Mr. Snow is a walking, talking snowman! Build some snow friends for him. Does he have a snow pet?

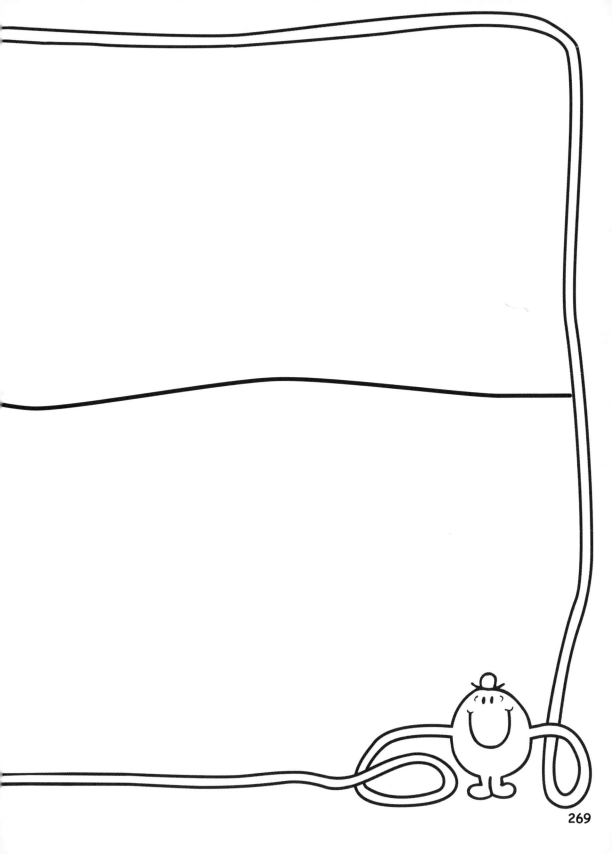

269

DOODLE FUN

Winter sports like skiing and snowboarding are fun. Add trees, flags, jumps, and more Mr. Men and Little Misses to the mountain. *Watch out, Mr. Bump!!!*

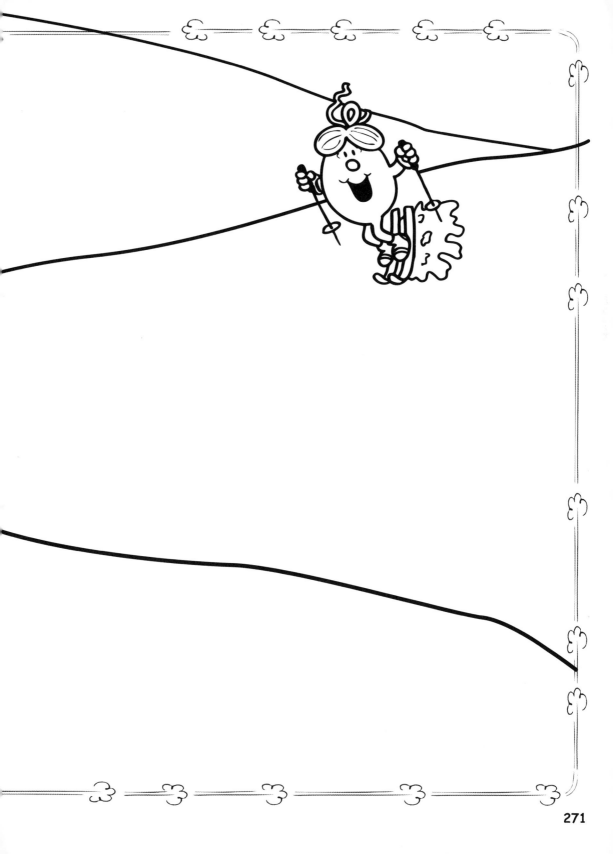

DOODLE FUN

It's a picnic! Draw the Little Misses enjoying lunch in the park. Give them everything they need for an afternoon in the sun!

DOODLE FUN

There's so much to do at the beach!
Give the Mr. Men and Little Misses everything
they need for a day by the ocean.

DOODLE FUN

Mr. Daydream is flying a kite! It's more fun to fly kites with friends, so draw some other Mr. Men to join him. How many kinds of kites can you design for them?

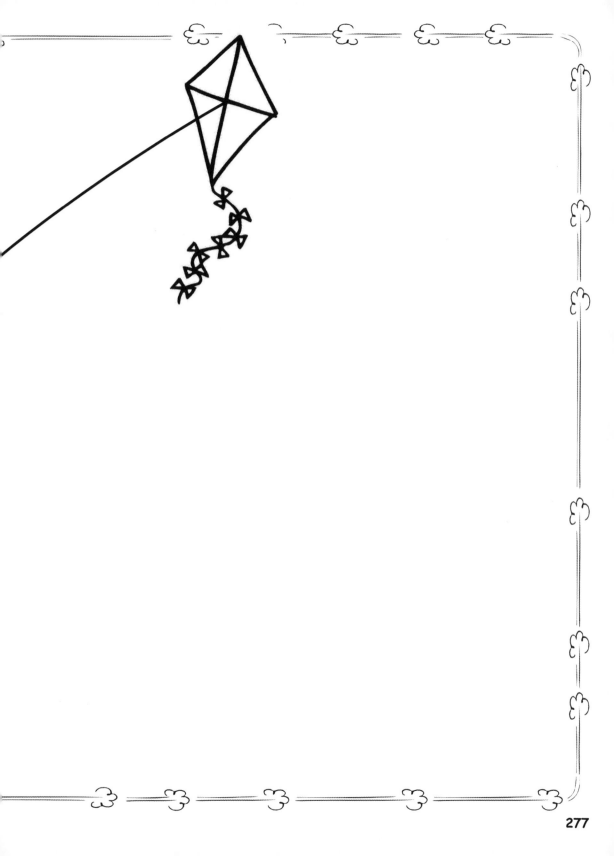

DOODLE FUN

Little Miss Trouble has won the contest
for the best sand castle! Draw castles for
the other contestants in the contest.

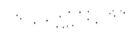

Mr. Tickle

Little Miss Scary

Mr. Messy

Little Miss Twins

DOODLE FUN

It's a beautiful day, and the Mr. Men and Little Misses are out on the water. Finish drawing their boats, and add some more of their friends. What animals might they see out at sea?

Little Miss Bossy

Mr. Muddle

Little Miss Trouble

Mr. Slow

DOODLE FUN

Fall is the perfect time to go apple picking!
Draw more trees for the Mr. Men and Little Misses
to pick from, and fill their baskets with apples.

Mr. Bump

Mr. Tall

Mr. Tickle

Little Miss Sunshine

Mr. Nosey

Little Miss Trouble

DOODLE FUN

It's time to trick-or-treat! Put costumes on everyone, and don't forget to give them bags to hold their candy!

Little Miss Chatterbox

Mr. Worry

Mr. Funny

Little Miss Shy

Little Miss Trouble

Little Miss Fun

Mr. Nervous

DOODLE FUN

Mr. Good loves to fix things. What is he fixing now?
Draw some more tools to help him!

DOODLE FUN

What is Mr. Bounce bouncing on? Maybe he's bouncing off a diving board into a pool. Draw a picture to show what Mr. Bounce is bouncing on.

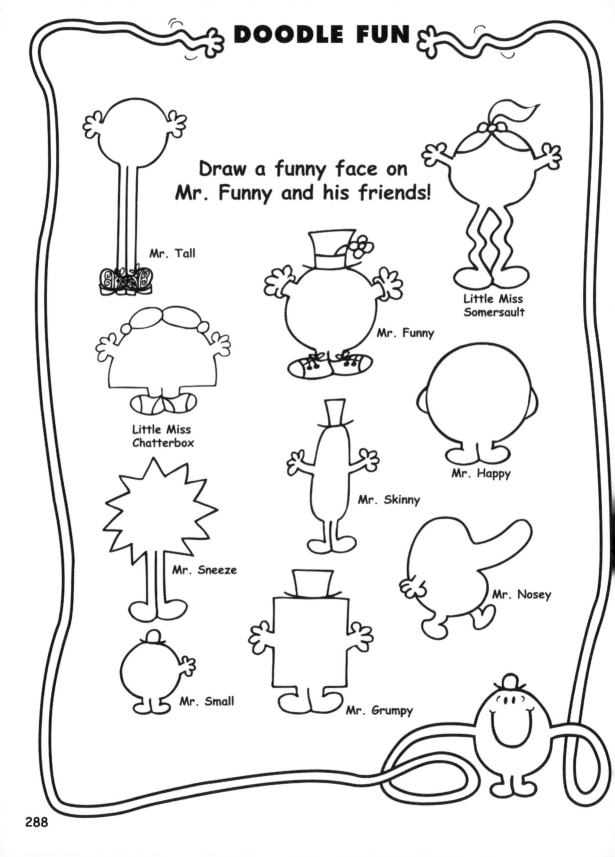

DOODLE FUN

Draw a funny face on
Mr. Funny and his friends!

Mr. Tall

Little Miss
Somersault

Mr. Funny

Little Miss
Chatterbox

Mr. Happy

Mr. Sneeze

Mr. Skinny

Mr. Nosey

Mr. Small

Mr. Grumpy

MR. HAPPY

by Roger Hargreaves

On the other side of the world, where the sun shines hotter than here, and where the trees are a hundred feet tall, there is a country called Happyland.

As you might very well expect, everybody who lives in Happyland is as happy as the day is long. Wherever you go, you see smiling faces all around. It's such a happy place that even the flowers seem to smile in Happyland.

291

All the animals in Happyland are happy as well.

If you've never seen a smiling mouse, or a happy cat or dog, or even a smiling worm—go to Happyland.

This is a story about someone who lived in Happyland, who happened to be called Mr. Happy.

Mr. Happy was fat, and round, and happy!

He lived in a small cottage, beside a lake, at the foot of a mountain, and close to the woods.

297

One day, while Mr. Happy was walking in those woods near his home, he came across something which was really very exciting.

There in the trunk of one of the very tall trees was a door. Not a very large door, but it was certainly a door. A small, narrow, yellow door.

Definitely a door!

"I wonder who lives there?" thought Mr. Happy, and he turned the handle of that small, narrow, yellow door.

The door wasn't locked and it swung open quite easily.

Just inside the small, narrow, yellow door was a small, narrow, winding staircase, leading down.

Mr. Happy squeezed his rather large body through the rather thin doorway and began to walk down the stairs.

The stairs went 'round and 'round and down and down and 'round and down and down and 'round.

Finally, after a long time, Mr. Happy reached the bottom of the staircase.

He looked around and saw in front of him another small, narrow door. But this one was red.

Mr. Happy knocked on the door.

"Who's there?" said a voice. It was a sad, squeaky sort of voice. "Who's there?"

Mr. Happy slowly pushed open the red door. There, sitting on a stool, was somebody who looked exactly like Mr. Happy, except that he didn't look happy at all.

In fact, he looked downright miserable.

"Hello," said Mr. Happy. "I'm Mr. Happy."

"Oh, are you really," sniffed the person who looked like Mr. Happy but wasn't. "Well, my name is Mr. Miserable, and I'm the most miserable person in the world."

"Why are you so miserable?" asked Mr. Happy.

"Because I am," replied Mr. Miserable.

"How would you like to be happy like me?" asked
Mr. Happy.

"I'd give anything to be happy," said Mr. Miserable.
"But I'm so miserable, I don't think I could ever be happy,"
he added miserably.

Mr. Happy made up his mind quickly. "Follow me," he said.

"Where to?" asked Mr. Miserable.

"Don't argue," said Mr. Happy, and he went out through the
small, narrow, red door.

Mr. Miserable hesitated, and then followed.

Up and up the winding staircase they went. Up and up and 'round and 'round and up and 'round and 'round and up until they came out into the woods.

"Follow me," said Mr. Happy again, and they both walked through the woods back to Mr. Happy's cottage.

Mr. Miserable stayed in Mr. Happy's cottage for quite a while. And during that time, the most remarkable thing happened.

Because he was living in Happyland, Mr. Miserable very, very slowly stopped being miserable and started to be happy.

His mouth stopped turning down at the corners.

313

And very, very slowly, it started turning up at the corners.

And eventually, Mr. Miserable did something that he'd never done in his whole life . . .

315

He smiled!

And then he chuckled, which turned into a giggle, which became a laugh. A big, booming, hearty, huge, giant, large, enormous laugh.

And Mr. Happy was so surprised that he started to laugh as well. And both of them laughed and laughed.

They laughed until their sides hurt and their eyes watered.

Mr. Miserable and Mr. Happy laughed and laughed and laughed and laughed.

They went outside and still they laughed.

And because they were laughing so much, everybody who saw them started laughing as well. Even the birds in the trees started to laugh at the thought of somebody called Mr. Miserable who just couldn't stop laughing.

And that's really the end of the story, except to say that if you ever feel as miserable as Mr. Miserable used to, you know exactly what to do, don't you?

319

Just turn your mouth up at the corners.

Go on!